WHAT IF I BREAK A BONE?

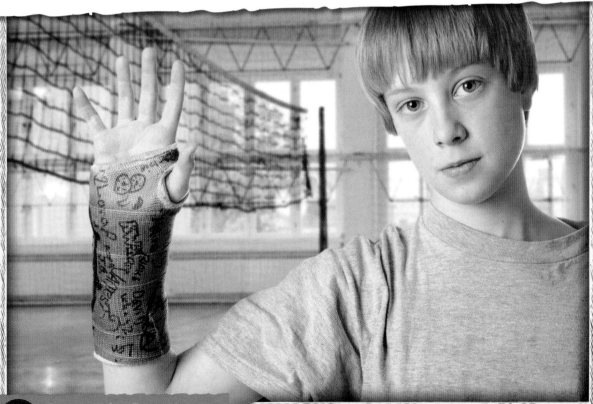

Gareth Stevens
PUBLISHING

 BY KRISTEN RAJCZAK NELSON

Please visit our website, www.garethstevens.com. For a free color catalog of all our high-quality books, call toll free 1-800-542-2595 or fax 1-877-542-2596.

Cataloging-in-Publication Data

Names: Nelson, Kristen Rajczak, author.
Title: What if I break a bone? / Kristen Rajczak Nelson.
Description: New York : Gareth Stevens Publishing, [2017] | Series: Benched: dealing with sports injuries | Includes bibliographical references and index.
Identifiers: LCCN 2015051085 | ISBN 9781482448917 (pbk.) | ISBN 9781482448856 (library bound) | ISBN 9781482448375 (6 pack)
Subjects: LCSH: Sports injuries–Juvenile literature. | Sports accidents–Juvenile literature. | Bones–Wounds and injuries–Juvenile literature.
Classification: LCC RD97 .N45 2017 | DDC 617.1/027–dc23
LC record available at http://lccn.loc.gov/2015051085

First Edition

Published in 2017 by
Gareth Stevens Publishing
111 East 14th Street, Suite 349
New York, NY 10003

Designer: Katelyn E. Reynolds
Editor: Ryan Nagelhout

Photo credits: Cover, p. 1 (background photo) dotshock/Shutterstock.com; cover, p. 1 (boy) Suzanne Tucker/Shutterstock.com; cover, pp. 1–24 (background texture) mexrix/Shutterstock.com; cover, pp. 1–24 (chalk elements) Aleks Melnik/Shutterstock.com; p. 5 SUSAN LEGGETT/Shutterstock.com; p. 7 Jodi Jacobson/E+/Getty Images; p. 9 Andrey_Popov/Shutterstock.com; p. 11 (inset) Hellerhoff/Wikipedia.org; p. 11 (main) itsmejust/Shutterstock.com; p. 13 (inset) travenian/E+/Getty Images; p. 13 (main) glenda/Shutterstock.com; p. 15 B Busco/Photographer's Choice/Getty Images; p. 17 Yellow Dog Productions/Iconica/Getty Images; p. 19 Tetra Images - Erik Isakson/Brand X Pictures/Getty Images; p. 21 (photo) Doug Pensinger/Getty Images; p. 21 (skeleton) Hein Nouwens/Shutterstock.com.

CPSIA compliance information: Batch #CS16GS : For further information contact Gareth Stevens, New York, New York at 1-800-542-2595.

CONTENTS

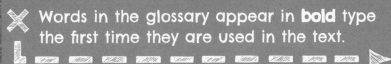

Words in the glossary appear in **bold** type the first time they are used in the text.

OUCH!

Imagine you're running toward the goal during a soccer game and step into a hole in the field. Your ankle turns at a funny angle and you feel—or even hear—a snap or pop. OW! You may have broken your ankle!

Don't panic! **Injuries** are a part of playing all sports. A broken bone, or fracture, may take a while to heal, but you aren't out for good. If you follow your doctor's orders, you'll be back on the field again soon enough!

✕ THE GAME PLAN

1 Sometimes other people can't tell how bad a fall you've had. If you feel something is hurt when you're playing a sport, tell an adult right away!

Breaking a bone can be scary, but know that your coach has probably helped other kids with injuries in the past.

JUST A SPRAIN?

If you think you may have broken a bone, stop playing immediately. It's possible you just have a sprain or strain. A sprain happens when the ligaments, or the body parts that hold bones together, tear or are **stretched** too far. A strain happens when a **muscle** or **tendon** tears or is overstretched.

Sprains and strains happen much like broken bones do. Often, only a doctor can tell you whether you have a broken bone, sprain, or strain.

✖ THE GAME PLAN

1. Mistaking a broken bone for a sprain or strain often happens at a joint, or a place where bones come together, such as a wrist or ankle.

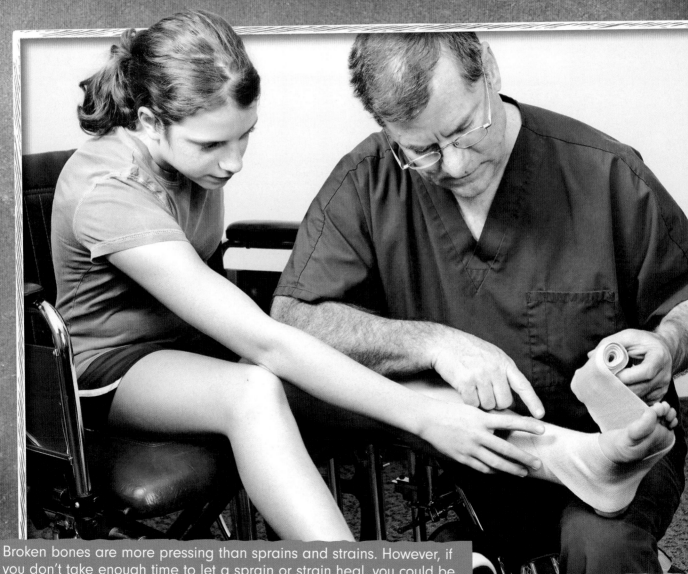

Broken bones are more pressing than sprains and strains. However, if you don't take enough time to let a sprain or strain heal, you could be more likely to reinjure yourself—and it could be worse the second time.

SIGNS OF A BREAK

If you've broken a bone:

» you hear a snap or grinding noise when injured.

» the injured area hurts, and the pain may get worse when touched.

» the injured area may have started to swell or **bruise**.

» your arm, leg, wrist, or other injured area might look like it's at the wrong angle or in the wrong spot.

» you might not be able to move the injured area.

» your bone may have broken through the skin.

Even if you only have a few of these signs, you should go to a hospital right away.

✖ THE GAME PLAN

If there's any chance you or a friend has broken a bone in your neck or back, have someone call 911. Don't try to move someone with this kind of injury!

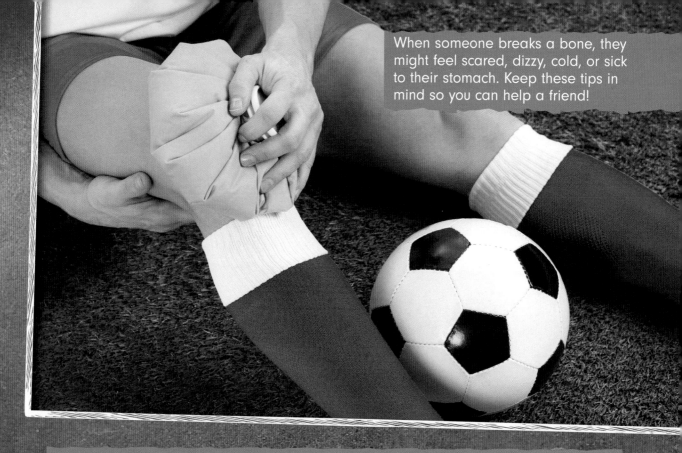

When someone breaks a bone, they might feel scared, dizzy, cold, or sick to their stomach. Keep these tips in mind so you can help a friend!

DEALING WITH A BROKEN BONE

stay calm

call 911
if no adults
are around

tell an adult

put towels or pillows
around the broken
bone to keep it still

put ice
on the
injured area

if possible, elevate
the injured area
to stop swelling

BONE PICTURES

In order to best help you, your doctor will have you get an **X ray**. You'll learn what bone is broken, where it's broken, and how badly it broke.

Kids' bones are a little softer than adults', so they often don't truly break—they bend! When one side of a bone bends, but the side doesn't break, it's called a buckle or torus fracture. A bend in the bone that causes one side to break is called a greenstick fracture.

✖ THE GAME PLAN

Bones break when they're put under too much **pressure**. Depending on the pressure, angle, and other elements, a bone might break completely through, even in more than one spot.

This X ray clearly shows a broken arm.

greenstick fracture

GAME, SET, CAST

Many broken bones need to be put into a **splint** or cast. But first, the bones need to be set, or put back in the right place. This can hurt a lot, but it makes sure your bones grow back the way they should.

A cast or splint keeps the broken bone from moving so it can heal. Splints are used for less serious fractures or if the area around a broken bone is still too swollen for a cast. Casts are stiff, but soft inside next to your skin.

✖ THE GAME PLAN

1 Inside your cast, your body is making new **cells** and **blood vessels** to close the spot where the bone is broken.

If you've broken your foot or leg, you might have a cast you can walk in and **crutches**. Walking with these takes some getting used to, but they keep weight off your injured foot or leg.

splint

BE PATIENT!

Casts for broken bones are commonly worn for 4 to 8 weeks. If you had multiple breaks or other injuries, the cast could be on for longer. Only your doctor can say when it's time for your cast to come off. In addition, only your doctor should take your cast off.

Once your cast is off, don't run straight to volleyball practice yet. Some injuries need "rehab," or rehabilitation. You'll work with people called physical trainers, who help you get stronger and practice moving normally.

✖ THE GAME PLAN

1. It might be itchy inside your cast. Putting a blow-dryer on "cool" and blowing it inside your cast will help!

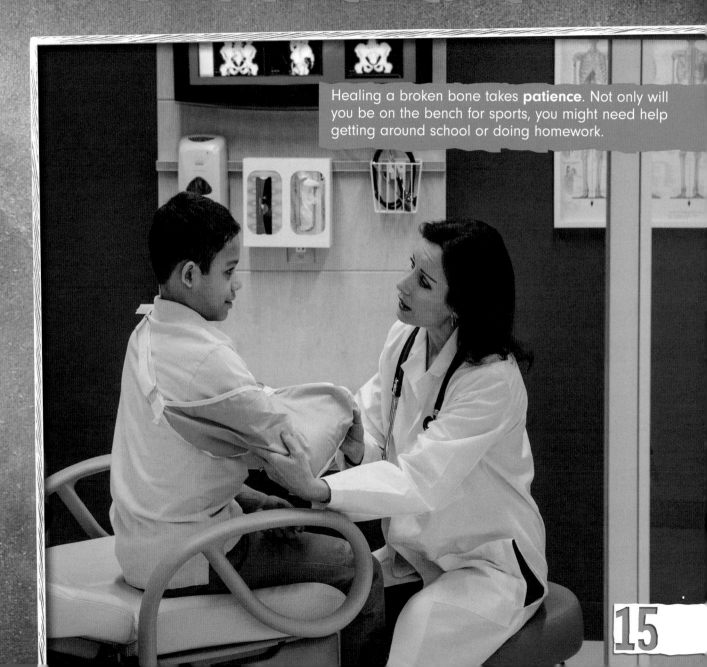

Healing a broken bone takes **patience**. Not only will you be on the bench for sports, you might need help getting around school or doing homework.

BACK ON THE TEAM

After you've broken a bone, it's exciting to head back to the gym, field, pool, or ice rink! The number-one rule, however, is to take it easy! The muscles around your injury will be weaker because you haven't been using them as much. Starting slowly will help prevent you from getting other injuries, like pulled muscles.

Your doctor will tell you when it's okay for you to start playing sports again. Doctors can also help you with exercises to strengthen the area you've hurt.

1 The place you've broken a bone isn't more likely to break again than other bones in your body.

It's normal to feel nervous the first time you head back to a team practice after an injury. Play smart, and you'll be back to your old self before you know it!

17

SAFETY

There's no sure way to keep from breaking a bone. But you can do your best! Most importantly, always wear the proper safety gear for your sport, including helmets, pads, and other clothing guards. They'll help you if you are hit hard and fall suddenly.

Just playing your sport makes it less likely you'll break a bone! Exercise is great for your bones. Foods with calcium and vitamin D in them are, too. These give your bones what they need to be healthy and strong.

✗ THE GAME PLAN

Leafy green vegetables, such as spinach and broccoli, and milk products, such as cheese and yogurt, all have lots of calcium.

Staying active is great for your whole body, not just your bones!

HOME PLATE COLLISION

On May 25, 2011, a runner **collided** with Buster Posey at home plate, likely on purpose. The San Francisco Giants catcher broke his ankle and tore several knee ligaments. It was the kind of injury that ends a season—and maybe even a career.

Posey had surgery 4 days after the collision and walked on crutches for months. But by 2012, he felt positive: "As hard as I've worked to get back behind the plate, I want to catch for as long as I possibly can."

THE FIVE MOST COMMON BROKEN BONES

collarbone

arm

wrist

hip

ankle

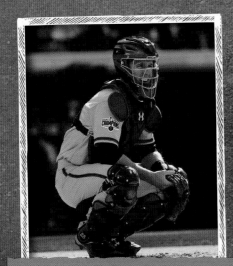

✗ THE GAME PLAN

Posey's injury caused many in Major League Baseball to push for change. Today, catchers aren't allowed to block home plate from runners, and runners can't go out of their way to hit a catcher.

GLOSSARY

blood vessel: a small tube in the human body that carries blood

bruise: a break in blood vessels beneath the skin that forms a dark mark

cell: the smallest basic part of a living thing

collide: to hit at a high speed with great force

crutches: supports that fit under the armpits and aid in walking

injury: hurt or loss to the body

muscle: one of the parts of the body that allow movement

patience: the ability to wait

pressure: a force that pushes on something else

splint: a stiff piece of metal or plastic joined to cloth and used to keep a part from moving

stretch: to reach across

tendon: a band of tough tissue that connects muscles and bones

X ray: a picture taken using a type of energy somewhat like light that shows the bones inside the human body

FOR MORE INFORMATION

BOOKS

Basen, Ryan. *Injuries in Sports*. Minneapolis, MN: ABDO Publishing Company, 2014.

Herrington, Lisa M. *I Broke My Arm*. New York, NY: Children's Press, 2015.

Mason, Paul. *Your Strong Skeleton and Amazing Muscular System: Find Out How Your Body Works!* New York, NY: Crabtree Publishing Company, 2016.

WEBSITES

Bone Fractures
*cyh.com/HealthTopics/HealthTopicDetailsKids.
aspx?p=335&np=285&id=2916*
How does a broken bone heal? Learn more here!

The Facts About Broken Bones
kidshealth.org/kid/ill_injure/aches/broken_bones.html
Find out more about the types of broken bones and what happens when one breaks.

INDEX